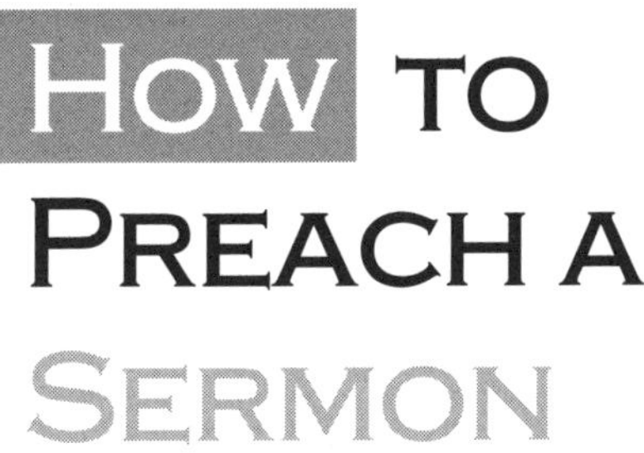

A Guide for the Amateur

Robert Slaughter

Skinner House Books
Boston

Published by Skinner House Books,
an imprint of the Unitarian Universalist Association,
25 Beacon Street, Boston, MA 02108-2800.

Printed in the USA.

Text design by Suzanne Morgan.
Cover design by Charlotte Burgess.

10 9 8 7 6 5 4 3 2 1
00 99 98 97

ISBN 1-55896-357-X

Dedicated to Ron Knapp

a preacher's preacher

Acknowledgments

Thank you, Ron, for letting me use your pulpit.

I have had the privilege of learning from a number of Unitarian Universalist preachers, notably Ron Knapp, Charles Stephen, Penny Binger, and John Weston.

Darrell Berg was my Methodist minister when I was a boy, during the civil rights movement. He risked his career for that cause, and taught me by example to say what needs to be said.

I am grateful to the congregation of First Unitarian Church for listening to me.

Many talented people at my church have taught and inspired me, including Mary Heise, Doug Paterson, Barb Ross, and John Whitehouse.

The Reverend Sarah Voss patiently read and commented on the manuscript. She was very helpful.

Contents

INTRODUCTION

SOMETIMES we talk ourselves into positions that have consequences we did not fully appreciate when we began talking. It was just such a situation that led me into preaching. Ten years ago I would have found the notion of Bob Slaughter in a pulpit laughable. For most of my life I have lived quite free of religion, even with a disdain for it. As a boy, I had a chance to be a Methodist, but at the wise age of thirteen I decided that I was an atheist and assiduously avoided anything that so much as suggested religion.

I did fairly well at life, enjoying a career as a medical doctor. But at the age of forty I began seeking and searching. A Catholic friend, after many attempts to convert me, suggested I attend First Unitarian Church in Omaha. I was delighted to find such a church, one that did not require me to make a creedal statement. Slowly, step by step, I became more and more involved.

I began to admire the many excellent preachers who came through First Unitarian Church, and I made a conscious effort to study their craft. Soon I was entertaining a Walter Mitty fantasy: me up there in the pulpit, speaking profound truths, the congregation rapt. They would besiege me with praise. Book offers and speaking engagements would follow—maybe a movie.

When I was elected president of the church, a scheme came to mind that would allow me to preach a sermon in reality. I would write a sermon, put it in a box at church, and wait for a scheduled preacher to get sick at the last minute or have a flat tire on the way to church. That was bound to happen sooner or later, and as president, I would not be out of line taking charge and filling in. This would be ideal. No one would expect a stellar sermon on five minutes' notice. Even a mediocre sermon would win me praise for saving the day.

Months went by as I waited for my chance. No luck. Unitarian ministers are a hardy, dependable lot. But another opportunity soon presented itself. Ron, our minister, announced a sabbatical, planned well in advance. When this rolled around, we would have to do about fifteen services on our own. By this time, I had written four sermons, so I offered all of them. It would be a bit more threatening to give a sermon announced in advance, but I would be scheduled among other amateurs, and besides, it was way in the future. I started telling everybody how great my sermons were, to get support for giving them during Ron's absence.

Then fate intervened. One Monday night I got a call. A terrible car accident had occurred, and Ron and his wife were at the hospital. I left word that I would help however I could, and that I would take care of things at church. I worried about Ron and tried to plan how the church would run in his absence. I figured that at least I had enough material to get us by for four weeks.

On Tuesday, I got word through the church secretary that Ron and his wife were badly shaken and bruised, but that they would be all right. Ron's van was totaled, but he was well enough to perform his duties. I breathed a sigh of relief.

But, as in the title of the soap opera, the world continued to turn. On Thursday, Ron called me at my office. As is frequently the case with car accident victims in the first few days, he was feeling worse and worse. Even over the telephone, it was clear that he was in a great deal of pain. Could I do the service on Sunday? he asked. I told him I'd handle it, that he should concentrate on getting well.

It was the understudy's dream: the star was sick on such short notice that there would still be a full house. But I had been a most boastful understudy, and in ninety-six hours, it would be show time.

I went into high gear, making all the logistical preparations. I called the church secretary to determine what he needed for the order of service. I called the organist to coordinate music with her. Immediately after work, I drove home, got my best sermon, and drove to church. It was dark outside, and the building was dark. I turned on all the lights in the sanctuary, turned on the sound system, and performed the entire service, everything except the music. On Saturday, I dragged a friend to church and checked all the sound levels: from the back, from the lectern, from the pulpit. I pressed my most conservative suit, polished my shoes, and set two alarm clocks. At 11:30 that night, I wrote these words:

> Tomorrow, I will do the church service . . . basically whatever happens tomorrow is my responsibility. First Unitarian is a century and a quarter old. I follow not only Ron, but . . . others who did services for a living, and did them impeccably well. I don't know why I am not more nervous. I have done all I can to prepare, and I continue to think about tomorrow, but it's not consuming. I am relaxed. . . . For what I am about to do, let fortune be truly helpful.

The next morning, I got to church early, powered up the sound system, put my reading text on the lectern, put my sermon text in the pulpit, made sure I had hymnals and orders of service where I needed them, and checked to make sure there was fresh Sterno in the chalice. Then I positioned myself in the foyer and prepared to greet people as they came in. I had been doing this regularly as president of the church, so no one suspected that anything was different. I greeted a speech teacher, two ministers, two radio announcers, and the chair of a university drama department. I became profoundly aware that I was not going to fool this congregation. We were all about to find out whether I could preach.

I did the opening reading from the back of the church,

which did not raise any eyebrows because Ron frequently has someone else do the opening reading. But when I read the affirmation, which Ron always reads, people began to suspect something. During the announcements I told the congregation about Ron's accident and said that I would preach in his place. Now everything was up front.

Finally, the time came to deliver the sermon. I was sitting alone at the front of a packed sanctuary, and I alone was expected to make it happen. I got up from the chair behind the lectern, where I had done my readings, and I crossed the front of the church. I paused at the bottom of the steps leading up to the pulpit and, just for effect, took my coat off and tossed it on a chair. Then I took the pulpit.

And I got up there and I did a good job. As the congregation filed out, I was awash in praise. People asked for copies of my sermon. It was one of the most rewarding days of my life.

Since then, I've preached a number of other sermons. In the process, I have learned a bit (mainly from excellent mentors like Ron) about how to write an effective sermon, and how to deliver one. You, too, can do this. You may never be the Unitarian equivalent of Billy Graham (interesting to contemplate), but with a little bit of work and practice, you can preach effectively. A sermon is an art form, like oil painting or photography. As such, it uses several general techniques and skills, regardless of its subject or point of view. My aim in this book is to teach you these skills.

As you learn to speak well, you will come to be in control of a powerful tool, useful for good or evil. It is a profound experience to wield the awesome power of oratory. When your time comes to experience this, you will understand how important it is not to abuse it.

I have organized this book into two sections, one about writing sermons and the other about preaching them. The title of this book mentions only preaching a sermon, but like many things, a resounding sermon springs from a lot of work before the product is unveiled.

I hope I can inspire some of you to have as much fun as I have had, and to make the world a better place by sharing your knowledge and inspiration.

Writing a Sermon

Starting Out

A SERMON is a unique form of communication. A person gets up and talks for about twenty minutes. The talk is self-contained: there are no slides, blackboard, or other visual aids. Unlike a talk at a convention or political rally, no subject is presumed. There are no assistants or panel to help the speaker. The audience participates only by listening. This is unusual in our world of visual media, where graphic illustrations, carefully edited action, and special effects abound. It is also unusual in terms of the length of time involved. We are used to much quicker messages, such as the politician's thirty-second "sound bite."

To make sermons work, you will need to write good material. This takes time: a good rule of thumb is to spend one hour writing for every minute you plan to speak. It also requires the right tools. It is a good idea to have a dictionary on hand (I am used to *The American Heritage Dictionary*), as well as a thesaurus (I have a *Roget's*). A thesaurus provides lists of synonyms for common words, which is helpful to keep you from using the same words over and over. Besides, synonyms never mean exactly the same thing, and you may find one with a shade of meaning that fits your purpose better. Many word processors incorporate a dictionary and a thesaurus.

Before you start writing a sermon, it's a good idea to review the components of the worship service in your church and to think about the role you will play. In my church, for example, the typical order of service goes like this:

Prelude	About three minutes of quiet music is played on the organ.
Opening reading	The person leading the service or a helper does a brief reading from the back of the sanctuary to set the tone of the service.
Lighting of chalice	A member of the congregation, chosen before the service, comes forward, lights the chalice, and reads the first line of a responsive reading from the order of service. The congregation responds with the second line.
Doxology	A brief, four-line hymn is sung. The tune is always the same, but the words can vary. This is a holdover from the Protestant liturgy.

Affirmation	An affirmation, generally of values widely held among us, is read together from the order of service.
Hymn	The congregation sings a hymn.
Announcements	The leader welcomes everyone and makes the announcements.
Offering	The morning offering is taken, accompanied by quiet, instrumental music.
Reading	One or more readings are done by the leader or a helper. These are usually the works of persons other than the leader, and serve to illustrate and introduce the sermon. The total time is approximately ten minutes.
Special music	An instrumental or vocal musical selection is performed.
Sermon	The sermon is given by the leader. It usually is about twenty minutes in length.

Hymn	The congregation sings a hymn.
Closing words	The leader gives the closing words, which are usually brief and dramatic. This corresponds to the Protestant benediction.
Musical response	A moment of quiet, contemplative music is played.
Postlude	The closing musical selection is played, which is frequently loud and joyous.

Of course, the order may be different in your church, but you'll need to make sure you are familiar with the routine and find out what you need to do in the way of supplying readings, coordinating music, and so on.

Structure

Whether you are speaking at your own church or as a guest, it is advisable to address the congregation informally at some point in the service. If you are a guest speaker, the beginning of your sermon is an appropriate time to thank your host, compliment them on their hospitality, praise the beauty of their sanctuary, and, if you have been a guest there before, say how happy you are to be back.

When you are on your home turf, you can usually incorporate any necessary chit-chat into the announcements and just preach when it's time to preach. Whichever approach you choose, you will have to command the congregation's attention for a sustained period of time once you start your sermon.

I once heard that a sermon should make three main points. I don't take that rule too seriously: a good sermon can make a single point or a plethora of suggestions, though it is best to avoid trying to cover too much ground or haranguing a preconceived notion to death.

I have my own three-point checklist. I think there are three things most good sermons do:

1. A good sermon must entertain. If you are boring, all else is lost.

2. A good sermon must inform. Obviously, you have to tell the people something they did not already know, or at least put a new spin on it.

3. A good sermon must inspire.

The last point, inspiration, is generally what makes a sermon a sermon, rather than merely a lecture. It is desirable to evoke awe. Awe is hard to define, but you know it when you experience it. You feel moved. You feel you have a new perspective on the world: a new way of looking at things, a new way of integrating the facts and your emotions. You feel that you know yourself and the universe a mite better. *The American Heritage Dictionary* defines awe this way: "A mixed emotion of reverence, respect, dread, and wonder inspired by authority, genius, great beauty, sublimity, or might." If you inspire that, you can really preach.

There is a fourth thing that *every* good sermon does: it must develop. A sermon that develops is like listening to a thoughtful person consider an issue and come to a conclusion about it. A sermon that does not develop is like listening to a zealot state a thesis, and then illustrate it with example after example. Such a sermon will usually have those who agree nodding, and those who disagree nodding off (or annoyed). A sermon that does develop, however, can change minds.

For instance, I recently gave a sermon on race relations in the United States. My ideas were well thought out, but I knew they would be controversial. I could have stated them forcefully, and used the rest of the time to appeal to those who agreed with me to begin with. That would have made those in my camp feel good, but it might have angered those who disagreed. They might wonder if they really liked going to a church that made them unhappy on Sunday morning.

Instead, I gave the sermon a rather ambiguous title, "Not as Clear as Black and White." I began with an excerpt from Martin Luther King's "I Have a Dream" speech, and I said that his goal was my goal. I drew on my experience as a medical student during the seventies when my training consisted of accompanying a social worker doing case work in the projects of Omaha, Nebraska. The projects were racially integrated, but most of the households we visited were black. I compared the racial situation during King's time with the situation I had observed in medical school. Then I offered my ideas. Finally, I returned to King's principles. Some people agreed with me and some did not, but no one was angry. Maybe I helped improve our society a bit. In any event, the service was much more productive, inspirational, and pleasant than it would have been had I taken an authoritarian, divisive tack.

In another recent sermon, I wanted to demonstrate that I have gained a greater appreciation of the spiritual in recent years, which I think is a good thing. But I did not state this up front and then give examples. I entitled my sermon "Second Looks: The Earth and Spirituality," and I delivered it in two parts. The first part was called "A Second Look at the Earth," and I gave it in the place in the service usually devoted to readings. I began by contrasting the beautiful, frame-filling picture of the earth that the *Apollo* astronauts took from space on the way to the moon in 1972 to a more recent picture of the earth taken from space. In the second picture, taken by the unmanned *Voyager I* from the edge of the solar system, the earth is only a pale blue dot. I wrote some inspirational stuff about that, which was not hard, but just for insurance, I put in a lengthy quote from Carl Sagan.

The second part, called "A Second Look at Spirituality," was given during the regular sermon time. I began by contrasting myself in 1972 and today. In 1972 I was unable to appreciate the first photo because I was excessively devoted to rationalism, but today the two images fill me with emotion. Next, I told a personal story. When a biblical question came up prior to my recent enlightenment, I recalled, I could not find my Bible. I had received a Bible at my confirmation as a teenager, but the overly rational young man of 1972 left it to be auctioned off with the rest of his mother's junk when she died. So I looked at the Gideon Bible in my office. Then, I bought a new Bible. In the process of looking up what I needed to find out, I was spiritually inspired. Then, I remembered a Bible I had had all along, but had forgotten: a 200-year-old family Bible. As a teenager, I rescued this

Bible from what was left of my grandmother's house after a serious fire. In it were recorded the high points of a teenage marriage that lasted thirty-five years and yielded eleven children. Three of the children died before adolescence. Imagine, I said, the emotions of those who held and wrote in this book.

I held up each Bible as I mentioned it, and though my congregation is largely not Christian, the effect was pretty inspirational. Some personal comments and a good story completed the journey. I didn't just tell them what I had figured out; I told them *how* I figured it out, and how I felt about it.

Even though you want your sermon to flow naturally, it is a good idea to go over what you want to cover before you start preaching, and to summarize at the end. It also does not hurt to say when you are finished with one topic and are moving on to the next.

For example, I recently gave a sermon about the book *What Your Minister is Afraid to Tell You About the Bible*, by Terry Cain. After telling a joke and introducing the book, I said, "I'm going to give my comments in three parts. First, I'll tell what I learned about the Bible from Cain's book; then I'll describe the theology Cain derives from the Bible; and, finally, I'll tell you what this means to me as a Unitarian Universalist." The rest of the sermon might be outlined as follows:

1. What I learned about the Bible from Cain's book.

Transition: "That's what Cain's book taught me about the Bible. Now, I'd like to say a few words about the religion Cain derives from the Bible."

2. Description of Cain's theology
   Transition: "Now I've told you what Cain taught me about the Bible and about his religion. What does all this mean to me as a Unitarian Universalist?"

3. Analysis of how Cain's book and theology relate to Unitarian Universalism, followed by moving closing story.

In most cases you should err on the generous side when giving clues as to where you have been and where you are going. After all, a sermon has no table of contents the listener can refer to. Indeed, the listener may not even have noted the title you gave your sermon. That is what I mean when I say a sermon is self-contained; it consists of what you say and nothing else. However, there will be times when you do not want to hand out clues; you may want the listener to pay attention and try to fathom what you are developing. It can be dramatic and suspenseful to omit such road signs, as I did with the sermon on my spiritual development, but it is also more difficult to pull off.

It's especially important to sum up effectively when you get to the end of your sermon. Your last two minutes must have everyone listening, and must evoke the awe experience. Get serious. You have just taken twenty minutes of a lot of busy people's time. As you sum up, you must convey the impression that you are absolutely convinced that they spent their time well. If you can't write profoundly good copy, you can end with a story or with a quote from someone who does write movingly. The sermon that I began by describing the pictures of earth from space could have ended with any one of many moving quotes by Carl Sagan. I could have ended my sermon on race with an excerpt from King's "I Have a Dream" speech. When you hear a quote or a story that you think would make an effective ending, save it. Sometimes a good ending will be flexible enough to work with quite a number of different sermons.

Whatever you do, though, *don't run long*. It's rude: consider the shy person in the congregation who has another commitment, but is reluctant to disturb others by walking out. At my church, the custom is a twenty-minute sermon and an hour-long service. On my first outing, my sermon ran twenty minutes, but everything else was short, so the service ran only forty-five minutes. Nobody complained. On the other hand, I've seen services run five minutes long, and everybody was restless.

You can estimate how long a service will run by calculating the length of each part and adding them up. Some parts, such as the doxology, always run about the same time. You can rehearse and time the length of other parts such as the readings and the sermon, and musicians can provide a good estimate of how long they will play. At my church, announcements must be approved in advance by the leader of the service. We do not schedule time for "joys and concerns" to be announced. However, we have a very liberal policy concerning inserts and announcements printed in the order of service, and the leader will draw attention to these items. Allowing anyone to contribute what they want during the service can undoubtedly build community, but it makes it impossible to guarantee an ending time.

Topics

When I first decided to write a sermon, I was stymied because I could not decide on a topic. Then, one night, we had a catered dinner at the church. One of the caterers, who I suspect was a Christian Fundamentalist, appeared to be quite uncomfortable simply being in the building. She looked about as if in fear, with a frown on her face. "What kind of church *is* this?" she asked. One of our members gave her a little talk on Unitarian Universalism that assuaged her fears sufficiently to convince her that brief exposure would not put her soul in jeopardy.

As I listened, a light came on. How many times had I been asked similar questions when I had said I was a Unitarian Universalist? "What do you people believe?" "Do you believe in God?" I quickly wrote a sermon on how I answered these questions—what I think Unitarian Universalism is, and what I think it should be. The experience taught me that if you want to write sermons, you should constantly be on the lookout for topics. If you read an inspirational book, think, "can I write a sermon based on that book?" If you are out enjoying nature and have a particularly beautiful experience, ask yourself, "can I get a sermon out of this?" If you are at a difficult point in life and find thoughts that comfort or ways to cope, there is a sermon there that will help others in a similar situation.

In a more traditional vein, many sermons are just waiting to be preached on our Unitarian Universalist heritage. The story of Norbert Capek and the flower communion he instituted just following World War I, can be told in so many ways. Francis Dávid wrote one of the first statements of religious freedom in human history; Jon Hus was burned at the stake for his religious beliefs and inspired the symbol of our denomination, the flaming chalice.

Our Judeo-Christian heritage, too, is as rich a source as one could imagine. At Christmas time, you can relate the story of the virgin birth of Jesus—almost certainly myth, but a fascinating myth. Or if you do not like that myth, you can relate the Hanukkah story. At Easter, you discuss the Resurrection or the story of Passover. Do not be too eager to reject these sources just because you do not believe the stories in a literal sense. Probably a lot of liberal rabbis and Protestant ministers do not either. At least many of them probably consider the metaphorical spiritual content of these stories to be more important than their literal truth. Have lunch with one of these folks. Tell them where you are coming from and what sort of message you want to convey. They can help you use these stories as a vehicle.

You can also use politics or social policy as the basis

of a sermon, and indeed I have done so, but I tend to tread lightly here. I keep my comments general, I avoid dogmatic statements of position on controversial issues, and when I do take a position, I offer it as a suggestion to be considered, rather than as a profound truth. Most Unitarian Universalists believe in the separation of church and state, after all. I also feel that a sermon does more when it inspires thoughtful consideration than when it advocates a specific position. The privilege of the pulpit is just that, as there is no rebuttal. Advocacy of specific positions is better left for a venue where all viewpoints can be heard.

STORIES

STORIES, as my examples have shown, often play a crucial role in a sermon, especially at the beginning and the end. Stories probably have been integral to preaching for as long as people have tried to get points across, because storytelling is an extremely effective means of communicating. Once, I attended a program about storytelling. We sat in a circle, and to begin, the leader asked that we each give our name and relate a brief story about our relatives. I said, "I'm Bob Slaughter, and I'm the grandson and the great-grandson of two women, each of whom lived to be a 101." When we were done, the leader pointed something out. Though we could not remember each other's names, we could remember each other's stories!

There are several types of stories. Some are true tales that simply convey the facts of history; a sermon about Unitarian Universalist notables would make use of this technique. The idea here is to give your listeners information of interest to them.

Another type of true story is the personal example. Here, the history is not as important as the principles it illustrates. When I gave my sermon on Terry Cain's book

What Your Minister is Afraid to Tell You About the Bible, for example, I wanted to create a bridge between my Unitarian Universalism and Cain's Methodist Protestantism. I described how Darrell Berg, the minister of the Methodist church I attended as a boy, risked his career by speaking out for civil rights in the late 1950s in a large, affluent, all-white church. Although I was sitting in a Methodist church, I was hearing common principles that I practice today as a Unitarian Universalist. Presented with appropriate drama, this topic was powerful stuff. A few well-chosen words about principles transcending doctrinal trifles, and we were into the closing hymn in good order.

But not all powerful stories are drawn from Life: in a lot of religions, Christianity included, parables are where it's at. A parable is a story that makes no pretense of being true. It may be, but it doesn't make any difference, because the purpose of a parable is not to relate what happened, but to illustrate a point. Look at the story of the good Samaritan (Luke 10:25-37). A lawyer is pulling Jesus' chain, nit-picking about exactly what Jesus is trying to teach. Instead of going over all his principles again from the top, Jesus tells a story: Some guy gets mugged and is lying in the ditch. Two people walk by but do not want to "get involved." The Samaritan, though, goes out of his way to help. "Now do you get it?" one can imagine Jesus saying.

When I gave my sermon "Second Looks: The Earth and Spirituality," I ended with a parable demonstrating that some spiritual concerns transcend particular religious dogmas. The ending went like this:

> The story happens at a rabbinical school. One of the teachers, Rabbi Abraham, was particularly admired by the students. His insights into the Torah and the Talmud were astounding. Curiously, he always disappeared for a couple of hours each afternoon, and it was rumored among some of the younger students that during this time he rose up into heaven and talked with God, just as the original Abraham had done, receiving there his awesome understanding.
>
> The students finally could not contain their curiosity and picked one of their number, Isaac, to follow the teacher. Isaac did his job well. Without detection, he followed the great teacher as he left the school one afternoon and walked deep into the neighboring woods, carrying a basket. They came upon an old, one-room dwelling. Rabbi Abraham entered with the basket, and Isaac hid himself where he could see inside through the sole window. He saw an old, bedridden woman whose face came alive with joy as the Rabbi approached and took her hands in his.
>
> Then he moved to a part of the room Isaac could not see. Soon smoke arose from the chimney, and

in a few minutes he reappeared at the old woman's bedside, now with a hot meal which he gently, spoonful by spoonful, helped her eat. When the meal was done, the Rabbi sat and read to the old woman for a while, then he lovingly laid his hand on her forehead and took his leave.

When Isaac returned to the school, he was besieged by his classmates. "Isaac," they asked, "did Rabbi Abraham rise up toward heaven?"

"Yes," replied Isaac, "he did rise up. He rose up farther than you can imagine."

I cannot remember where I heard that story, but it ended the service on such an effective note that I wished I could have taken up the collection *after* the sermon instead of before!

Parables abound in secular writing as well; think of Aesop's fables. And, of course, you can write your own parables. If you do so, though, it is best not to take credit for them. Simply say "let me tell you the story about the . . . ," rather than "let me tell you this story I wrote about the. . . ." One reason parables are so effective is that listeners are allowed to imagine that the stories came from some great source of wisdom, far away and long ago. You and I, on the other hand, are very fallible humans, standing right there for all to see. If you are not intentionally misleading your listeners, I think it is all right to allow them to imagine some remote or lofty source for your story.

Finally, there are Bible stories. Obviously, you do not have to have a Bible to write a sermon for Unitarian Universalist audiences! But if you get traditional in your middle age as I have, and you want to draw from this rich source, then you will have to choose which translation to use. The one that comes closest to modern language is the New Revised Standard Version, and I highly recommend it. (The Living Bible is even closer to contemporary language, but it is more of a paraphrase.)

If you really want to sound "biblical," use the King James Version. It is the one everybody who was raised Christian grew up with. Catholic versions of the Bible have a few extra books, called the apocrypha, which are lacking in Protestant versions. Also useful is a concordance, a reference book that lists all the places a given word occurs in a particular translation of the Bible. You also can get the Bible on CD-ROM for your computer.

LET ME TELL you a story. At one point in my life, I was going out with a woman who was a member of the Wisconsin synod of the Lutheran denomination. The synods of the Lutheran denomination are a curious thing. Anyone who has studied Protestant Christianity is aware that Protestants are divided into a vast array of different denominations, with widely differing beliefs. Well, the synods are to Lutheranism what the denominations are to Protestantism.

At one end of the spectrum are the ELCA (Evangelical Lutheran Church in America) Lutherans, a pretty reasonable bunch of folks who just happen to hold the teachings of Jesus to be a lot more important than most Unitarian Universalists do. One can discuss things with ELCA Lutherans; my office manager is one. The Missouri synod Lutherans, on the other hand, are fundamentalists; that is, they believe that the Bible is the inerrant, literal word of God. I find this concept, and a good deal of the political agenda the Christian Fundamentalists attach to their religion, very hard to defend.

Go a few steps further, and you have the Wisconsin synod Lutherans. When my significant other joined a

Wisconsin synod Lutheran church, I knew I was in trouble. We actually got along, though, for a surprisingly long time after this happened. On Sunday mornings, she would go to her church, I would go to mine, and we would get together for lunch, where I would ignore her occasional reminders that I was destined to burn in Hell for all eternity because I did not "believe."

This routine was upset one year when Christmas fell on a Sunday. At my church we canceled church, figuring people would want to be with their families. This blew my friend's mind. I suggested that I could go to church with her; after all, I'm open-minded and tolerant. She could not refuse because this was an opportunity to "save" someone, no matter how remote the odds.

So we showed up on Christmas morning at my friend's church. The building was tiny, and the congregation numbered about thirty. Most of the service was a set liturgy, read out of a book, which I was told was the same every week. There was a sermon, appropriately for Christmas, on Jesus. Perhaps it was paranoia, but the minister seemed to look right at me as he roared "Jesus is deity!" (The nature of Jesus was a major sticking point between the early Unitarian Christians and their Trinitarian colleagues.) When it came time for communion, I was not tempted to participate, but if I had been, I would have been forbidden by the note in the order of service stating that communion was available only to Wisconsin synod Lutherans; this to create a more "God-pleasing" ceremony. These people seemed to claim to know God better than I know my next door neighbor!

On the way out, seeking some common ground between our two churches, I asked my friend if they had coffee hour after church. No, I was told, "we have Bible study." (That, fortunately, had been canceled for Christmas, or I would have gotten into a lot of trouble.) The minister was shaking hands at the door. My friend introduced me. The minister looked me straight in the eye and growled, "WE'RE GLAD YOU'RE HERE."

That is the end of my story. In my church, I used it to start a discussion on how Unitarian Universalism is open and tolerant. I really hammed it up, particularly the last line, which I read in a very gruff, authoritarian voice. Then I paused a moment, made a Hyde to Jekyll transformation, smiled charmingly, and said, "Well, here at First Unitarian, we don't want to change you. We really *are* glad you're here, just the way you are." This is an example of how humor can get a sermon off to a good start. After an opening like that, the congregation is ready to listen to you talk.

Opening humor doesn't have to involve a long story. When I preached a sermon inspired by a book I had read, for example, I observed that it's common to use a book as the basis for a sermon. Then I lightheartedly accused our minister of preaching sermons based on books he had not read. Ron, I explained, could do that, because he has "natural preaching ability." As for myself, I went on, I had to *read* the book I was going to talk about.

The material for an opening joke is limited only by your imagination. One time, I was sitting in the front of the church while a guest minister was in the back, poised to do the opening reading. As I perused the order of service, I noticed that one of the guest minister's readings was from the Bible. Recalling an embarrassing incident with another guest minister, I suddenly realized that he might expect to find a Bible in the pulpit. Trying to look like it was absolutely the most appropriate thing to do, I walked to the back of the church and asked the guest if he needed a Bible. He did not, but the fact that I asked (evidently with a look of sheer panic) became the humorous anecdote with which he began his comments!

Most of us cannot prepare humor on such short notice, and indeed we should not try. Write your funny stuff ahead of time. At my church, we are privileged to have among our members one "Otis XII," who makes a living by being funny. Otis is the DJ on a very successful "drive to work in the morning" program. He leads a team of three announcers who just seem to spontaneously make one funny remark after another. If you get Otis aside, though, he will admit that a lot of rehearsal goes into his humor. One time Otis was going to do a church service on humor in religion. I was going to do the announcements, so I touched base with him the evening before. The service was all ready to go, he said, except that he still had to write the sermon. He invited me to tell any jokes I wanted during the announcements.

The next morning the service got off to a good start.

I actually got a few laughs during the announcements, but I was completely overshadowed when Otis began his supposedly last-minute sermon with the following story:

> Cantor Feynman ran into a friend of his, Joshua. "How are you doing, Joshua?" he asked.
>
> "Not so well," replied Joshua. "Not so well. My son has converted to Christianity."
>
> "Oy!" said the cantor. "My son, too! We must go talk to Rabbi Simon." When they had located the rabbi, Cantor Feynman explained the situation. "Rabbi Simon, both Joshua and I have tried to bring up our sons in the tradition, but both have converted to Christianity! What are we to do?"
>
> "Oy!" replied the rabbi. "My son, too! We must pray."
>
> "Dear God," he prayed, "all of our sons have converted to Christianity! What are we to do?"

At this point Otis cranked his voice up to full blast, obviously speaking as God:

> "OY!! MY SON, TOO!!!"

The point of Otis's sermon was that it is funny how doctrinal quibbles and ceremonial concerns can obscure the meaningful aspects of spirituality. He was off to a good start.

PREACHING
A SERMON

Of course, writing and planning a sermon is one thing; actually delivering it before a crowd of people is quite another. It's understandable to be nervous, but it helps to be prepared. As you will see, this requires a lot of foresight about details that you may have taken for granted when you sat among the congregation, but it is not too complicated once you know what you are getting into.

Sound systems are a new thing. Up until a few decades ago, people who spoke had to rely on the power of their voice, and a strong voice was probably a requirement for becoming a preacher. Imagine doing a service in one of the big cathedrals in Europe. It's really inconceivable that one could be heard for an hour without amplification. Maybe that's why there was a fixed litany—the same words said each time and memorized as part of catechism. Many sermons given at my church early in this century were published in the newspaper. Maybe one went to church for the beauty of the ceremony and read the sermon later.

You, however, will most likely preach your sermon where there is a sound system, so you need to learn how to speak into a microphone. It might not be fair, but if you can work the sound system well, you will appear professional. If you make a stupid error, everyone will know you are an amateur.

So practice this ahead of time; the first time you preach for real, you will have enough on your mind without worrying about how to work a microphone. Arrange a time when you can have the sanctuary to yourself. Have a friend sit about a third of the way back. Turn on the sound system and read something. Do not be self-conscious. Read loudly, read softly, position the microphone in various different ways, get close to it, move back from it—try everything. The first thing you will discover is that it is very hard to tell if the microphone is picking up your voice or not. That's what your friend is there for. Pretty soon, you will figure out where to position the microphone, and where to position yourself, so you can be heard. Note all this, and also note how all the controls are set on the amplifier. Then, having done all you can, forget about the sound system until it is your day.

When that day arrives, bring or recruit someone to serve as a plant in the congregation. Their job is simple. If you are too loud, they hold a finger in front of their lips. If you cannot be heard, they cup their hand behind their ear. Before the service, check out the sound system by turning everything on and speaking at each microphone. Have your plant tell you how you sound. Do not be embarrassed to do this. I have done some services with a member of my congregation who is a professional radio announcer, and he *always* checks the sound system at the beginning of the service.

Modern microphones are very sensitive: if you get your mouth too close to the microphone, it will make an explosive noise when you say the sound of the letter "P." Try doing this on purpose when you practice, and you will find out just how far back you have to stay to prevent it from happening. When you test the sound system before the service, you can say "Peter Piper picked . . ." instead of "test; one, two, three," just to make sure you are all right.

Be very careful not to bump the microphone with anything; it will make an unbelievably loud noise. Be very gentle adjusting the microphone when it is on, and handle the pages of your text as quietly as possible.

If you have to move away from the microphone for a moment—say to pick up a prop—you will appear very professional if you have the presence of mind to quit talking when you are out of the microphone's range.

One thing some people do not consider on their first time out is that if you stay near the microphone when a hymn is sung, your voice will be heard over everyone else's. If you have a good singing voice, it's wonderful to lead the congregation in song; if not, move back a couple of steps.

Remember that the sound system, once you turn it on, amplifies everything said near the microphone. That includes casual conversation and humorous comments intended for a limited audience. More than one professional has lived to regret a remark that was unknowingly made within a microphone's range.

Cues

A RELIGIOUS service runs smoothly when all the people involved know their cues. If you are preaching at your home church, chances are this responsibility will fall to you. Your church probably has a routine order of service, and you should not stray far from it.

What you need to do is talk, just before the service, to each person who will play a role, and make sure they know exactly what their cue is to begin, and exactly what cue they need to give when they are finished to prompt the next person. If you can talk to everyone at once, this only takes about two minutes. It takes just a bit longer if you have to catch the participants as you can. It's as simple as that, yet too often unnecessary slip-ups occur because this is not done. Do not hang back for fear of appearing too assertive; people generally want to know exactly what is expected of them, and they will enjoy being a part of an organized service more than a chaotic one. Even the best actor or actress appreciates a good director.

Let's return to the sample order of service that I outlined earlier. This is the system we usually use in my church. On the right is the information that would need to be shared for cueing. Pat is Pat Will, our organist, and I am Bob:

Prelude	Pat starts at 11:00 A.M., after making sure Bob is in the building.
Opening reading	Reader 1 does this when the prelude ends, having been duly warned by Pat that the prelude has two movements. At the end, Reader 1 says, "Please stand for the lighting of the chalice."
Lighting of chalice	Those words prompt the Chalice Lighter to light the chalice and lead the responsive reading.
Doxology	Pat starts when the Chalice Lighter is done.
Affirmation	Bob starts this at the end of the doxology.
Hymn	Pat starts at the end of the affirmation.
Announcements	At the end of the hymn, Bob tells everyone to sit down, and does

	the announcements, ending with, "The offering will now be received."
Offering	On those words, Pat starts playing, and ushers take the collection.
Reading	When the music stops, Reader 2 does the reading.
Special music	Pat starts when Reader 2 sits down.
Sermon	Bob starts when the music stops. At the end, Bob nods to Pat.
Hymn	On that cue, Pat starts the hymn.
Closing words	Bob starts at the end of the hymn. Bob has warned Pat that the closing words have some dramatic pauses. At the end, Bob nods to Pat.
Musical response	On the nod, Pat starts.
Postlude	Pat starts four counts after the end of the musical response.

The first service I did involved only Pat, myself, and someone who helped with one of the readings, and it was strictly in our standard service format. Pat and our minister Ron have been doing this for more years than I have been around (Pat was very precocious as a musician). After I had gone over all our cues at least three times, Pat looked at me and said, "Bob, I'm a professional." I looked back, probably with terror in my eyes, and said, "I'm not!" Pat was most supportive that day, and always has been.

What to Take to the Pulpit

I DO NOT KNOW what Billy Graham takes to the pulpit; likely nothing more than his Bible. And, of course, he mesmerizes literally millions with great ease. But you and I are not Billy Graham. What do we need to take with us? There are basically three possibilities: take nothing at all, take notes about what you want to say, or take the text of your talk.

If you take nothing at all, you will be speaking "off the cuff." You have probably seen people speak effectively at some length with no notes, and seemingly with no preparation, but before you try it, think about the circumstances under which you have seen this done. It is a frequent device in the movies. Imagine a typical scene: Injustice is prevailing. Our previously quiet heroine/hero, suddenly struck by a sense of moral urgency, jumps up and delivers a well-organized, comprehensive, and persuasive discourse on the matter at hand. But that is the movies. The playwright probably spent days writing this "spontaneous" talk.

You also may have seen professional preachers, usually evangelical Christians, pull this off. But I do not advise trying to emulate them, at least not at the start.

First, you do not have their skill or experience. Second, your message likely will be a more complicated and novel one than salvation through faith, and this will require a more prepared, organized approach. If you ultimately find you are gifted enough to go to the pulpit with no notes and can move a congregation as Oral Roberts does, invite me to hear you.

At the other extreme, you can go to the pulpit with the text of your sermon written out word by word and read it. This is, as a matter of fact, the way most effective sermons are given. Writing your sermon down will force you to do the proper research, organize your thoughts, and come up with the very best wording you are capable of. I highly recommend this, at least for your first outing. No matter how nervous you get, and no matter what happens, you can read one word after another. The only disadvantage of this approach is that many us sound rather wooden when we read from a text, but there are ways to combat that. A big advantage, on the other hand, will become apparent when you really knock them dead and people ask for copies of the sermon to send their friends.

An intermediate approach, one between taking word-by-word text to the pulpit and taking nothing at all, is to take notes to the pulpit. This is safer than speaking off the cuff, because you do have to organize your thoughts, and you have something to rely on if you get nervous. At the same time, your speech will likely sound more genuine than it might if you were reading.

This approach lends itself well to an interactive, "feel free to interrupt me with questions any time" format; I have given many lectures on technical subjects this way. But that is not (at least traditionally) the format of a sermon. A sermon is supposed to be a carefully assembled packet of knowledge handed to the listener without hesitation and with no loose ends. So I have always given my sermons from verbatim text.

I have had an opportunity to compare giving the same talk from notes and from text. A little while after I got into the sermon business, I had occasion to write a talk for groups who wanted to know about Unitarian Universalism. I wrote it down word-by-word, but then I got to thinking. What if there were only a few people? Then it would be quite rude to ask people to hold all questions until the end, as would be appropriate with a large audience. So I decided to make a little card of key phrases that I could use to give the talk more informally, with questions and discussion welcome at any point.

I practiced my talk both ways, and I learned two things. First, I could read the talk in less time than I needed to from notes. Consequently, text may be the way to go when there is a time constraint. Secondly, I felt that my message was more effective when I read than when I spoke from notes. I lost a little bit of sincerity and eye contact, but my improved organization and choice of words more than made up for that.

If you do decide to read your sermon verbatim, it's a good idea to run off a copy with one-and-a-half or even double line spacing, to make it easier to read. It's too easy to lose your place reading single-spaced copy. Before the service starts, you should place this copy on the lectern, on the right-hand half of the platform. Now, make eye contact, take a deep breath, and start reading. Use your left hand as a marker to keep track of which line you are on. As you gain experience, you will not have to do this all the time, because you will develop a subconscious habit of noticing where you are on the page when you look up. But your first time up, do not hesitate to use your hand as a guide throughout the entire sermon. No one will notice you are doing this, but they will notice if you lose your place. Having only one hand to gesticulate will not be too much of a handicap; you probably will not be getting that carried away until you have more experience.

When you begin to near the end of the first page, move it, still right-side up, to the left-hand half of the lectern. Then, you can shift your eyes from the first page to the second, just as if you were going from the bottom of one page in a book to the top of the next page. When you get done, all of your pages will be in the left-hand pile, face up, with the first page on the bottom, and the last on the top. All of this can be reversed if you are left-handed, of course. This system eliminates the risk of hitting the microphone when you turn pages.

People who wear bifocals may notice a special problem reading in the pulpit: the copy lying on the lectern may be too close to see through the top part of the lenses, yet too far away to see through the bottom part. As an eye doctor, I can assure you that this problem can be solved, but you will have to mention your special need when you are examined for glasses.

Another problem that comes up in reading from the pulpit is maintaining eye contact with your audience. You might think that in order to appear sincere, you would have to look at the congregation almost all the time, stealing only an occasional glance at your copy. Actually, the opposite is true; you can look at your copy most of the time, giving the congregation brief, but frequent, glances. That's all it takes. I'm old enough to remember when newscasters read the news from pages on their desks. Of course, they had not had time to memorize their copy. All they could do was steal quick glances at the unforgiving lens, but it was enough to make you feel they were reading the news just for you.

Now, things have changed. Newscasters have TelePrompTers and computer monitors set into their desks. The purpose of these things is to make it easier to maintain eye contact while reading. You, however, will have to do things the old-fashioned way. One thing you can do, though, is to try to arrange things so you do not have to raise your eyes through so great an angle to go from your copy to the congregation. You can do this by raising the lectern if it is adjustable, by standing back from it a bit, and by placing your copy near the front edge of the lectern. It also helps to be short, but you really cannot plan that.

I remember one night I was up late working on something in my den, and I had the television on. One of those "infomercials" came on; you know, one of those program-length commercials. The announcer was trying to sell religious audio tapes. I caught glimpses of the program, and it seemed like the guy was pretty good, so I resolved that I would watch if I saw the infomercial again. Sure enough, they ran it again. It was about fifteen minutes in length, and consisted of the salesman speaking from a set that resembled a living room with chairs, a sofa, and a fireplace. As he spoke, the man stood up, walked around, leaned on the mantel, sat down, and so forth.

As near as I could tell, the entire program was filmed in a single take, with no editing, and with one camera. The amazing thing was that the announcer never, not for an instant, broke eye contact with the camera! If he was using any type of prompter, I could not pick up on it. Having dealt with the problem of eye contact while speaking, I could appreciate this man's abilities. But the fact is that those of us with more ordinary abilities can also deliver most effective talks.

Like a lot of things, your preaching skill will improve with practice, and probably will *not* be very great until you *do* practice. You need to hone your skill before your big day comes and continue to practice on a regular basis if you want to get better. It is easy to develop a habit of reading aloud one page a day, which takes about two minutes. Put the text of your next sermon in a convenient place and read one page a day at some time in your daily routine. I put mine on the ironing board in my den at home and practice first thing when I get home from work. An ironing board makes a fine practice lectern, but any high, flat surface would serve. You want to practice standing up to make the situation as realistic as you can.

If possible, try to practice when no one is around. Really ham it up so you can see what works and what does not. Most beginners, understandably, tend to be inhibited; when you are alone you can let it all hang out. Then, when the time comes, you will have the confidence to show the kind of emotion that distinguishes a sermon from a lecture. Sometimes it's fun to read the same line more than once, emphasizing different words and pausing in different places just to experiment with the effects you can create. Gradually, you will find yourself sounding more and more like a sincere preacher, and less and less like an amateur reading text.

You will make mistakes, such as stumbling on a word,

or losing your place. When this happens, *do not stop*; try to recover as gracefully as you can, just as if you were in front of people. Everybody makes mistakes, so recovering is part of effective preaching. Knowing you can do so will help you maintain your composure when you bobble a word in front of a real congregation. When you are practicing, though, go back and try the line again. If you consistently err at the same place, mark the passage to warn yourself to slow down and proceed with caution.

Just as you need to practice recovering from mistakes, you must learn to ignore distractions. In church, you will need to be able to go on without missing a beat when a baby starts to cry, or a fire engine goes by with its siren wailing. (It is another matter if it stops in front of the church!) So if the phone rings while you are practicing or the doorbell rings, or the cat knocks your coffee over, *keep talking*. You do not have to go on very far, just a sentence or two. Then you can stop and attend to things. One's natural tendency is to stop talking when distracted and to proceed only after the distraction has been tended to. When preaching, you will need to do the opposite: do not stop at a distraction unless a good reason becomes apparent.

People who are professionals at speaking take pride in being hard to distract. One of my mentors, a retired radio announcer, recalls nights when he and a colleague were alone in the station and had to do everything themselves. They would take turns doing the news, which was provided by a wire service and printed out by a teletype on a roll of paper. When they were busy, they did not have time to edit, so when the news segment came up, one of them would have to tear off whatever had come in since the last news segment, go to the microphone, and edit while reading so the listeners would hear a smooth presentation. This, he said, represented the epitome of the announcer's art, as the text could easily be six feet long, and the news segment was only three minutes.

Gradually a competition arose between the two professionals to try to distract and fluster each other when they were reading the news. My mentor proudly stated that the listenership never detected the slightest waver in his voice, even when his colleague quietly walked into the studio and set the bottom of his text on fire!

Another thing to practice is the way you move your hands and body as you speak. Everyone has a mental picture of a hellfire-and-brimstone Fundamentalist minister putting the fear of God in his congregation. Such a minister raises his hands in prayerful appeal to God above, shakes his fist at the Devil below, waves his hands in expansive motions of evangelistic fellowship to his congregation on earth, and cries when he contemplates his woeful inadequacy in the eyes of God. His congregation shouts "Amen," and "right on, brother," and, from time to time, a worshiper will fall into a trance, have a seizure, or begin to speak in tongues.

I do not agree with the theology of such ministers, and I suspect you do not either, but we can learn from them. They do indeed impart an overwhelming spiritual experience to their followers. I used to admire the sermons of more religiously "liberal" ministers who substituted the controlled presentation of a reasoned argument for the emotional appeal of the Fundamentalist ministers, but one can go so far to the side of rationalism that spiritual and ceremonial needs are neglected. However "rational" or "liberal" your congregation, they still want to be moved.

I suggest that you watch some Fundamentalist ministers and just go with the emotional flow. Watch their body language. Notice that compared to the way you would gesticulate when making a point in coffee-hour conversation, preachers exaggerate everything.

Consider, for example, the way you would gesticulate when expressing incredulity—the fact that you do not agree with something and, indeed, find it ridiculous. Suppose some religious order has proposed making its teachings part of the public school curriculum, and you vehemently disagree. At coffee hour, you go over all the religious order's arguments for having its views become standard fare for our school children. Then you express incredulity by saying, "Does that make sense?" As you say this, you maintain eye contact with your listener, but you turn your head a bit to one side. You lift your eyebrows slightly, and your shoulders go up in a faint shrug. You turn your hands palms-up. All those nonverbal signs tell your listener that your question is a rhetorical one; you definitely do not think it "makes sense."

By coffee-hour standards, you have been rather forceful, but this won't do when you're in the pulpit. The words are all right, but the gesticulations could stand some work. From the middle of the sanctuary, your eyebrow level will be imperceptible, and your hands will be hidden by the lectern. So here is what you do. Memorize the line "Does that make sense?" and the next few words, so you can maintain eye contact with your listeners while making your big point. When the big line comes, raise your hands to shoulder level, palms up, and shake them. Shrug you shoulders maximally, scrunch your face up in righteous indignation, and, moving your head, pan the entire room with your gaze. Now, *that* will be forceful by pulpit standards.

Of course, this requires the confidence that can only be gained through practice, so experiment in private. Your confidence will grow, and you will start trying some of these things when you are "live." Your congregation will love it.

Reading Dialogue

Because storytelling is such an important part of preaching, you will often find yourself reading dialogue—that is, a conversation between two characters. This can present a problem, because you will usually be working with a text that was written to be read off the page by individual readers, not to be read aloud from a pulpit. The reader, unlike the listener, has clues to distinguish the dialogue from the narrative: the dialogue is in quotation marks, and it is good form to start a new paragraph when a different person speaks. When you read something aloud, those clues are lost.

Let me give an example. Here is some written dialogue:

> Bill and Mary had been driving for a long time. "I'm tired," said Bill. "Let's stop for the night."
>
> Mary sighed. "We could make Bakersville. What's before that?"
>
> "I don't know."
>
> "Well, then, let's try to make Bakersville."
>
> "I'm pretty tired."
>
> "Bill, if we get to Bakersville, we can stay at my aunt's."

"OK," conceded Bill, "but you drive."

You can follow that if you can follow a dime novel. But what happens if we remove the punctuation and paragraph clues? This:

> Bill and Mary had been driving for a long time. I'm tired, said Bill. Let's stop for the night. Mary sighed. We could make it to Bakersville. What's before that? I don't know. Well, then, let's try to make Bakersville. I'm pretty tired. Bill, if we get to Bakersville, we can stay at my aunt's. OK, conceded Bill, but you drive.

As you can see, it is difficult to tell who said what. When you read aloud, you must somehow make up for the lost cues, lest you leave the congregation confused as to who is speaking. One thing you can do is to pause when one speaker finishes and another is about to enter. Another is to insert a few phrases like "Joe said" and "the angel replied" to keep it clear who is speaking. I think this is acceptable even when you are quoting directly, as long as the meaning is left unchanged. You can think of these additions as editorial comments, analogous to text that would be in brackets in a printed quote.

For example, here is how I read the story of the good Samaritan from Luke 10:25-37, which can be a little confusing, even in the New Revised Standard Version. The words I say in addition to the original text are in brackets, and [...] means a pause:

> Just then a lawyer stood up to test Jesus. [...] "Teacher," he said, "what must I do to inherit eternal life?" [...] He [Jesus] said to him, "What is written in the law? What do you read there?" [...] He [the lawyer] answered, "You shall love the Lord your God with all your heart, and with all your soul, and with all your strength, and with all your mind; and your neighbor as yourself." [...] And he [Jesus] said to him, "you have given the right answer; do this, and you will live."
>
> [...] But wanting to justify himself, he asked Jesus, "And who is my neighbor?" [...] Jesus replied, [...] "A man was going down from Jerusalem to Jericho, and fell into the hands of robbers, who stripped him, beat him, and went away, leaving him half dead. Now by chance a priest was going down that road; and when he saw him, he passed by on the other side. So likewise a Levite, when he came to the place and saw him, passed by on the other side. But a Samaritan while traveling came near him; and when he saw him, he was moved with pity. He went to him and bandaged his wounds, having poured oil and wine on them. Then he put him on his own animal, brought him to an inn, and took care of him. The next day he took out two denarii, gave them to the innkeeper,

> and said, 'Take care of him; and when I come back, I will repay you whatever more you spend.' Which of these three, do you think, was a neighbor to the man who fell into the hands of the robbers?" [...] He [the lawyer] said, "The one who showed him mercy." [...] Jesus said to him, "Go and do likewise."

Try reading this aloud. See how the pauses make it clear when you are at the end of a quote. In just a few places, it is not clear whether it is Jesus or the lawyer speaking. You can figure it out when you read it to yourself, but you do not want your listeners to have to figure it out; with just a few inserted words, it's crystal clear.

The first answer the lawyer gives is interesting, by the way. It's usually read with great feeling, as it's pretty heavy-duty stuff within the framework of Christianity. I like to read it here rapidly, with a singsong lilt, as one would recite redundant legal verbiage. Read this way, it becomes clear that the lawyer already knows the answer, and is just pulling Jesus' chain. This makes Jesus' response a paradigm of patience. And the last line: memorize it and read it with full eye contact. You are not likely to come upon much better material, so make the most of it.

A fun thing you can do with dialogue is to read the different parts in different voices. The example below is from the children's book *The Velveteen Rabbit*, by Margery Williams. I read the part of the rabbit in falsetto (a voice teacher can show you how to do that), and the part of the skin horse in a low, croaking voice. I further embellished my storytelling by digging out a stuffed leopard that I took everywhere with me as a little boy. I introduced it before the story and put it on the lectern, where it sat throughout the service. Everything else, I did in my normal voice. I printed it as you see it below, so I would not get the parts mixed up:

"What is real?"

> asked the Rabbit one day, when they were lying side by side near the nursery fender, before Nana came to tidy the room.

"Does it mean having things that buzz inside you and a stick-out handle?"

> "REAL ISN'T HOW YOU ARE MADE," said the Skin Horse, "IT'S A THING THAT HAPPENS TO YOU. WHEN A CHILD LOVES YOU FOR A LONG, LONG TIME, NOT JUST TO PLAY WITH, BUT REALLY LOVES YOU, THEN YOU BECOME REAL."

"Does it hurt?"

> asked the Rabbit.

> "SOMETIMES," said the Skin Horse, for he was always truthful. "WHEN YOU ARE REAL YOU DON'T MIND BEING HURT."

"Does it happen all at once, like being wound up,"

he asked,

"or bit by bit?"

"IT DOESN'T HAPPEN ALL AT ONCE," said the Skin Horse. "YOU BECOME. IT TAKES A LONG TIME. THAT'S WHY IT DOESN'T HAPPEN OFTEN TO PEOPLE WHO BREAK EASILY, OR HAVE SHARP EDGES, OR WHO HAVE TO BE CAREFULLY KEPT. GENERALLY, BY THE TIME YOU ARE REAL, MOST OF YOUR HAIR HAS BEEN LOVED OFF, AND YOUR EYES DROP OUT AND YOU GET LOOSE IN YOUR JOINTS AND VERY SHABBY. BUT THESE THINGS DON'T MATTER AT ALL, BECAUSE ONCE YOU ARE REAL, YOU CAN'T BE UGLY, EXCEPT TO PEOPLE WHO DON'T UNDERSTAND."

This type of thing is a lot of fun, but you need to practice. Do not practice special voices for too long at a time, or you will get hoarse.

Here is another example that shows how special voices and gesticulation can work together to make a great story. I do not know where this story came from; I first heard it from John Whitehouse, a member of my church. The text of the story is on the right, and my suggestions for reading it are on the left. "Read normally" means to read as you would read the rest of the sermon—in your normal tone of voice, glancing up occasionally.

Read normally.	A Samurai warrior confronted an old Buddhist monk sitting in meditation.
Raise your hands in front of your chest. Adopt a ferocious expression. Speak in a gruff voice.	"Tell me the meaning of life!"
Read normally.	The monk did not break his meditation. The warrior kicked at the monk.
Read like the warrior's first line.	"Tell me now or you will die!"
Read normally, but keeping your eyes on your text.	The monk spoke softly, not raising his eyes. "Go away. You are not worthy to know."
Read normally, while using both hands to mimic an imaginary sword.	The warrior was furious and decided to kill the monk with a single blow of his sword.

Read normally, dropping your hands.	As his sword reached its apex,the monk remained motionless, staring ahead.
Read with normal volume, but with intensity, and keeping your eyes on your text.	"That!" said the monk, "is hate."
Read normally.	The warrior froze, his sword uplifted.
Read normally, but keeping your eyes on your text.	Slowly he realized the monk had risked his life to teach one he had not even looked upon.
Read slowly, while slowly raising your eyes to meet those of the congregation. Do not break eye contact from here on. Pause.	The monk's eyes rose slowly, and met those of the warrior.
Knock them dead!	"That," said the monk, "is love."

This story would be especially effective at the end of a sermon, when reading well is particularly important. It would make a great ending to a sermon on Buddhism, but it could also be used to end a sermon on nonviolence, or one on multiculturism.

Afterword

Fear of Speaking

One of the benefits of preaching is that your church is a relatively safe, friendly place to confront a fear that many people share: the fear of public speaking. The ability to speak effectively in public is one of the most valuable talents one can have, but it is closely tied to self-esteem. If your self-esteem is in order, you will not be afraid to speak, because even if you do not do well, you will still feel good about yourself. In the absence of self-esteem, however, public speaking is a tightrope. One slip, and you will feel totally inadequate.

When I was a little boy, I never worried about reading and speaking in class; it was easy. By the time I got to junior high, though, I was having a self-esteem problem: I was a nerd. Consequently, I was scared to death to get up and talk. I remember the dread Ordeal of the Book Reports. Each of us, said the sadistic English teacher, would be assigned a book. We would be given abundant time to read it (more time to worry), and then we would have to a give a book report on it. The ordeal lasted three days, one fifty-minute period each day. We sat like doomed men and women, waiting for our names to be called off in random order. Nothing terrible ever happened during book reports. But my fragile, adolescent ego was protected by a thin facade, and just the threat that it would be torn down, and all my perceived inadequacies laid bare before my peers, was agony.

Later, in medical school and specialty training, I perceived myself as pretty hot stuff. I had no trouble speaking to groups, and I was even invited to lecture to students, which I did well and enjoyed. When I went into private practice, I gave talks about my specialty, ophthalmology, to the public. I did pretty well at that, too, and I had no problem with fear.

Alas, fortunes change. A few years later, when I got involved in my present church, I was terrified of addressing the congregation. Fate had thrown some challenges my way, and I was no longer sure of my course in life. I had decided in advance to chicken out when the inevitable day came that our minister, Ron, selected me to light the chalice and lead the responsive reading. After all, those who lit the chalice could read perfectly; what if I made a mistake?

Then one day, Henry Lemon was called upon to light the chalice. Henry has been a church member for twenty-five years. Henry enjoys profound respect, gained through a lifetime of service as a doctor specializing in cancer treatment. He took care of my mother during her final illness, and he also taught me in medical school. As one would expect, Henry is an excellent speaker. He has, I am sure, delivered the responsive reading for the lighting of the chalice flawlessly, many times. On this particular day, though, Henry made a mistake; he stumbled over the words, and had to repeat himself.

Sometimes the smallest things can deliver the greatest messages, and this was one of those times for me. For nothing happened when Henry made a mistake—no bolt of lightning from on high, nothing. No one cared, least of all Henry, and I doubt anyone even remembered. This made me think. I resolved that the next time an opportunity arose for me to speak before the congregation, I would say yes. Then, I would just do the best I could. I realized that that was all that anyone expected of me, and all I should expect of myself.

It was not long before Barbara Ross asked me if I would say a few words at Christmas Vespers. True to my resolution, I said yes. Christmas Vespers is a tradition at my church. On the Sunday evening preceding Christmas, we have a lay-led service involving the children, with lots of music, and lots of the spirit of the season. Every year, it's a bit different. That year, Barb planned to have families get up and describe how the season is celebrated in their households. She had selected representatives of all different types of families. There was a traditional family with a working father and a stay-at-home mother who took care of the children. There was a blended family with each partner bringing children from a previous marriage. There was a single-parent household, and an older family whose children had all moved away.

I was supposed to speak for about three minutes as the representative for single people without children. I turned on my creativity. Indeed, Christmas can be a difficult day for those without family. Everyone else is with their family, and every place one might go to do something is closed. The year before, I recalled, I had planned so much to do that I was not lonely. But when lunchtime came, an interesting thing happened. I was pulling out of my driveway, on the way to the convenience store to get a sandwich, when along came a neighbor who is Jewish and lives alone. She hailed me and asked where I was going. She thought it was sad that I had to dine that way on our mutual non-holiday and invited me to her house, where we had a very delightful meal of canned tamales.

Now that's a good story, I think you will agree, and I wrote it up well. Then, I practiced it. And practiced and practiced and practiced it, until I had unintentionally memorized it. I decided I would give the talk from memory, with a copy of the text in my back pocket in case I needed it. Finally, the big night came. Although I had figured I would be speaking from behind the lectern, Barbara had a special microphone set up, in the style used by standup comedians. If I had to go for my crib notes in my pocket, I would have nothing to hide behind. And Barbara, bless her heart, had somehow placed a spotlight in the organ loft at the far end of the sanctuary, pointed at the spot where I would stand. It was one of those heavy-duty theatrical spotlights about the size of a civil war cannon, which project a perfect circle of blinding white light precisely on the subject, while all else is in darkness. And my circle of light would be the smallest of all, because I was the only one speaking alone.

I was beginning to wish I had just lit the chalice when I had the opportunity to. But I got up there, and everything went fine. It usually does when you do your homework. This is when I began, just began, to taste how sweet it can be to inspire through speech.

Join me. Put yourself together, put your thoughts together, and then share. Everyone will be richer.